GUIDELINES FOR CAVE AND KARST PROTECTION

IUCN - The World Conservation Union

Founded in 1948, The World Conservation Union brings together States, government agencies and a diverse range of non-governmental organisations in a unique world partnership: over 800 members in all, spread across some 125 countries.

As a Union, IUCN seeks to influence, encourage and assist societies throughout the world to conserve the integrity and diversity of nature and to ensure that any use of natural resources is equitable and ecologically sustainable.

The World Conservation Union builds on the strengths of its members, networks and partners to enhance their capacity and to support global alliances to safeguard natural resources at local, regional and global levels.

The Role of WCPA

The WCPA (World Commission on Protected Areas) is one of six Commissions of the IUCN. It is the World's leading global network of protected area experts with over 1000 members in 160 countries working in a voluntary capacity. WCPA promotes the establishment and effective management of a world-wide, representative network of terrestrial and marine protected areas. This is essential to ensure that protected areas can effectively meet the challenges of the 21st century.

Gordale Scar, Yorkshire Dales National Park, UK. (photo J. Watson)

GUIDELINES FOR CAVE AND KARST PROTECTION

World Commission on Protected Areas (WCPA)

Synthesised and edited by

John Watson
Elery Hamilton-Smith
David Gillieson
Kevin Kiernan

for the

WCPA Working Group on Cave and Karst Protection

IUCN - The World Conservation Union

1997

Published by

IUCN
The World Conservation Union

Environment Australia
Biodiversity Group

Citation: Watson, John, Hamilton-Smith, Elery, Gillieson, David and Kiernan, Kevin, (Eds.), 1997. *Guidelines for Cave and Karst Protection*, IUCN, Gland, Switzerland and Cambridge, UK. 63pp.

ISBN: 2 8317 0388 3

Printed by: Goanna Print, Canberra

Cover photo: Natural Arch near Chuan Yan cave, Guilin, Guanxi, China. (photo D. Gillieson)

Produced by: Environment Australia, Biodiversity Group P.O. Box 636 Canberra ACT Australia 2601

Available from: IUCN Publications Services Unit,
181a Huntingdon Road, Cambridge, CB3 ODJ, UK

or

IUCN Communications Division,
Rue Mauverney 28, CH-1196 Gland, Switzerland 28, CH-1196 Gland, Switzerland

CONTENTS

Appendices:

SCOPE OF DOCUMENT

The primary aim of these guidelines is to increase awareness of cave and karst protection issues primarily within the IUCN, WCPA and associated management and conservation agencies and with an emphasis on national parks and other protected areas.

The guidelines have been modelled as a 'sister volume' to 'Guidelines for Mountain Protected Areas' published by IUCN in 1992. Hence a similar format and level of detail have been used.

There are literally thousands of speleologists, cave explorers, scientists and managers around the world who have had the opportunity to contribute to earlier drafts of these guidelines. Conversely there are many thousands who for various reasons (*eg*. language difficulty, lack of access to electronic mail or facsimile) did not have the opportunity. Nevertheless, we are confident that the input received is reasonably representative and has contributed to a valuable set of guidelines at the level of detail that has been addressed.

Indeed, all comments received were very carefully considered and the great majority (over 600) incorporated to improve the text. There were, however, some major topics and issues raised which we were unable to address within the current scope of the guidelines, in particular:

- artificial cavities: this is a quite different issue, of considerable importance in any consideration of cultural heritage, but generally only linked with caves and karst because of superficial similarity and common techniques of exploration.
- lava tunnels and other pseudokarst: we believe it would be appropriate and valuable for another team to develop a separate volume which deals with volcanic landscapes including pseudokarst.
- contents of caves (*eg*., minerals, sediments, biota, palaeontological/archaeological/cultural heritage): we will examine this further, either as a second edition of this volume or as a companion volume.

Thanks are due to all the lead writers and all who commented upon early drafts or contributed in any other way towards preparation of these guidelines. On-going feedback on this volume after its publication will be appreciated by the Working Group and will be retained as input towards any future review or reprint.

John Watson,
c/o Department of Conservation and Land Management (CALM),
ALBANY,
Western Australia.
January, 1997.

ACKNOWLEDGEMENTS

First and foremost the lead writers must be thanked for undertaking the difficult task of preparing the first draft - David Gillieson, Elery Hamilton-Smith, Kevin Kiernan - and others who also contributed to the workshop held in April 1995 at Gowrie Park, Tasmania, namely Kevan Wilde, Andrew Spate, Nic White and Sue White. Comments or feedback on early drafts were received from:

Philippe Axell	Belgium
M Bakalowicz	France
Onac Bogdan	Romania
Eugenio de Bellard	Venezuela
G Deblock	Belgium
R Delfosse	Belgium
David Drew	Ireland
Brian Finlayson	Australia
Paul Griffiths	Canada
John Gunn	UK
L Haesen	Belgium
William Halliday	Hawaii
Paul Hardwick	UK
Ian Houshold	Australia
Chris Hunt	UK
George Huppert	USA
C Juberthie	France
John Lattke	USA
M Laumanns	Germany
V Maltsev	Russia
A Mangin	France
D Mattart	Belgium
Greg Middleton	Australia
Joep Orbons	Netherlands
Phillip Parker	UK
Adrian Phillips	UK
Graham Price	UK
Ivan Rubesa	Venezuela
David Sheppard	Switzerland
Dean Smart	Thailand
Andy Spate	Australia
Rob Stitt	USA
H De Swart	Netherlands
Jim Thorsell	Switzerland
M P Vevillez	France
Rauleigh Webb	Australia
Kevan Wilde	New Zealand
Wang Xianpu	China

There was also extensive informal and oral feedback from various others, including a group of delegates to the US National Cave Management Symposium held at Spring Mill, Indiana, in October 1995. The draft document was also field tested in 1995 by a group conducting a training programme with the National Parks Service of Thailand.

Coordination of the project since inception, and overall editorial responsibilities were undertaken by John Watson of the Department of Conservation and Land Management (CALM), Western Australia.

The Spanish translation was undertaken by John Lattke and Jorge Bontes, and the French by Philippe Axell and Florence Gerard, a French student who worked as a CALM volunteer in Albany during October, 1996.

Final editorial work and production were undertaken by David Gillieson and Ric Longmore of Environment Australia.

PREFACE

Karst landforms and associated features such as caves are distributed widely throughout the world. They have many values and many are located in various protected areas, including several which are on the World Heritage list.

Some reasons for their protection include:

- As habitat for endangered species of flora and fauna.
- As sites containing rare minerals or unique land forms.
- As important sites for the study of geology, geomorphology, palaeontology and other disciplines.
- As culturally important sites, both historic and prehistoric.
- As spiritual or religious features.
- For specialised agriculture and industries.
- As "windows" into understanding regional hydrology.
- As sources of economically important materials, especially groundwater.
- For tourism and its associated economic benefits.
- As purely recreational areas, both scenic and challenging.

These values may often be combined in a single cave area. For example, the Batu Caves massif in Malaysia houses a remarkable cave fauna which has been subject to research over virtually 100 years, and includes extremely rare and endangered species such as the segmented spider, *Liphistius*; it is also the home of a rich surface flora including various endemic species; it is the site of an important Hindu temple and has other important cultural values; it is a spectacular and readily accessible example of a karst tower; it is a recognised tourism attraction and also provides various recreational opportunities.

Karst and caves are indeed special places. They do however require special management considerations often extending well beyond the formal boundaries of any protected areas in which the more obvious features occur.

Appropriate management expertise does not usually lie solely within the formal protected area agencies - in fact there is probably no other landform type where such a high proportion of the specialised expertise lies *outside* such agencies, within the ranks of speleologists and cave explorers.

These guidelines have been prepared as a brief *"aide-memoire"* for planners, managers and users of the karst estate. They contain only generalised advice.

The examples used reflect the first hand knowledge of those who have volunteered time to contribute to their preparation. More specific guidelines and management plans for karst and caves will need to be prepared at national, area and specific site levels. The development of these should involve local communities.

An initial draft of these guidelines was prepared by a small group of speleologists and karst managers in Australia but with significant input and subsequent modification by other speleologists and protected area managers from around the world through the World Commission on Protected Areas (WCPA) Working Group on Cave and Karst Protection.

The Working Group is an informal network of scientists, managers, cavers and speleologists who see the need to improve the sharing of information and expertise between protected area managers, speleologists and other karst specialists. The group was formed at the Fourth World Congress on National Parks and Protected Areas held in Caracas, Venezuela, in 1992. It has subsequently provided advice on cave and karst management to protected area managers and others. It has also commented on several World Heritage nominations and it has prepared these guidelines - the first time such an overview has been produced at the global level.

We hope that the guidelines will make a significant contribution to our knowledge of the special management considerations essential for protection of caves and karst. They are a "first step" and the challenge now is for the national and site specific strategies to be developed in karst areas around the world. We also recognise that these guidelines can provide a basis for wider consultation, and in due course, the preparation of a more comprehensive and effective international document.

Adrian Phillips
Chairman WCPA
and
Jim Thorsell
Head, Natural Heritage Programme
IUCN, Gland, Switzerland
January, 1997

Buddhist shrine in Pak Ou Caves, Mekong River, Laos (photo R. Longmore)

I. INTRODUCTION : THE CONTEXT OF KARST PROTECTION

The protection of karst areas gives rise to various special issues which may be unfamiliar to many protected area managers. In particular, the boundaries of any karst system may be difficult to determine. It must be recognised that karst systems are effectively delineated by the total watershed area, of which the karst may be only a part, and further, that the effective subterranean divide which bounds such a watershed may be, and often is, quite different from the surface divide. This was not recognised when many existing protected areas were established. Effective management of many protected areas thus involves off-reserve lands, and the negotiation of conservation agreements with other owners or managers.

A contrast with mountain areas might be helpful here. A mountain area can be readily defined by topography, and can be considered virtually as an island which is only marginally impacted by what occurs in surrounding areas. Conversely, a karst area is generally much more like a lake or wetland in that it is massively impacted by whatever occurs on surrounding lands.

Further, many karst areas are of an immense size and often have high economic values. Although it must be accepted that the whole of such areas will not be assigned to parks or other protected areas, it again means that managers must often endeavour to negotiate appropriate conservation practices in adjoining lands.

The Planina Polje in Slovenia is an example of a karst landscape long used for agriculture. (photo G. Middleton)

II. KARST ENVIRONMENTS AND CAVE SYSTEMS

Karst landscapes represent an important facet of the Earth's geodiversity, and one of major management significance. The term *karst* denotes a distinctive style of terrain which is characterised by individual landform types and landscapes that in large measure are the product of rock material having been dissolved by natural waters to a greater degree than is the norm in most landscapes. In the narrow sense, the word refers to any area which has been shaped by solution processes. More broadly, it is an integrated, yet dynamic, system of landforms, life, energy, water, gases, soils and bedrock. Perturbation of any one of these will impact upon the rest of the system.

All rock materials are soluble to a degree, but the most fully developed karst is naturally to be found in the more soluble rocks. Hence, karst is generally most fully evolved in carbonate rocks such as limestone and dolomite and evaporite rocks such as gypsum (*eg*. in the Ukraine). Such rocks are present over about 30% of the earth's land surface but they vary in their susceptibility to karstification.

Given sufficient time and environmental stability, true karst phenomena may also develop in what are generally considered to be relatively insoluble rocks, such as quartzites and quartz-sandstones, while sculpturing by solution occurs in granite and related rocks.

Caves and other typical karst features may also result from other processes, and give rise to the phenomenon known as *pseudokarst* - land systems which contain karst-like features such as caves and surface collapses which are not formed by solution.

Examples include volcanic landscapes with lava tubes (tunnels), caves which have resulted from melting of ice in and under glaciers, in snowpacks or in permafrost terrain, caves resulting from tectonic movement, and caves which have been formed by piping or other mechanical processes in loosely consolidated sediments or under duricrust land surfaces. Many of the principles stated in these guidelines are also important in the management of pseudokarst landscapes; in general, wherever the term karst is used or implied here, the reader should recognise that it also includes pseudokarst.

In some environments solution processes are overwhelmed by other geomorphic processes such as glacial erosion, in others solution is more dominant. Karst areas are best known for the underground drainage systems or solutional cave systems that often evolve there, but may also be characterised by intricately sculptured rock surfaces (*karren*), blind valleys and closed depressions (*dolines, poljes, uvalas*), residual hills, cenotes, sinking streams and springs. However, karst may also be relatively flat and without striking surface features.

Figure 1. Schematic of the dynamics of the solution process in surface karst (Gillieson, 1996)

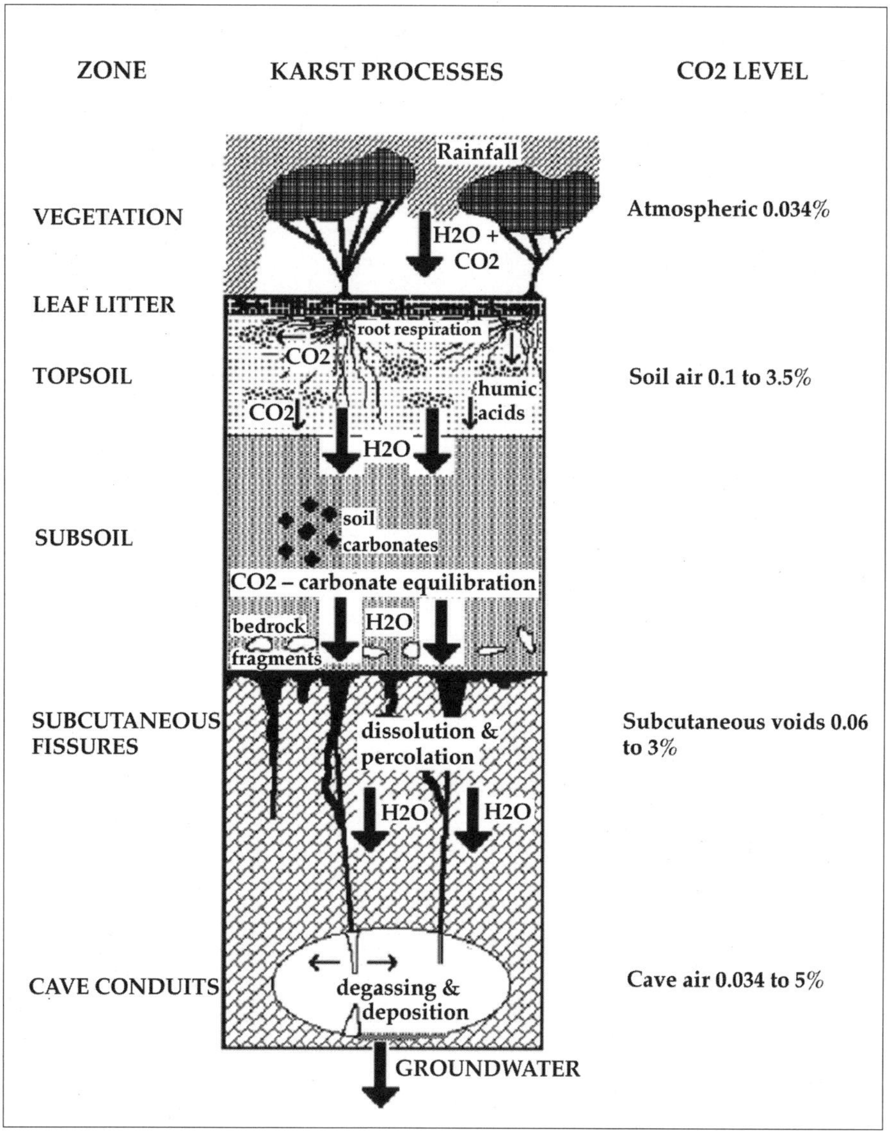

Figure 3.7 from Gillieson, D. Caves: Processes, Development and Management. *Copyright 1996. Reproduced by permission of Blackwell Publishers*

Polygonal karst landscape at Waitomo, New Zealand. (photo D. Gillieson)

Such landscapes can offer an extraordinary variety of economic, scientific, educational, recreational and aesthetic resources. But they are also potentially highly sensitive, comparable in this respect to coastal margins, lakes or other wetlands, and careful protective management is essential.

Two essential characteristics of karst must be taken into account in developing protective policies: its integrity is intimately dependent upon maintenance of the natural hydrological system; and karst is vulnerable to a distinctive set of environmental influences.

Millions of people live in karst areas, some of which are among the most spectacular landscapes on earth, but some have become highly degraded or permanently damaged. The availability of water is often a significant determinant of settlement patterns and water management has often been a major factor in the long term (or in extreme cases, even short term) survival of societies that dwell in karst regions.

Many karst areas have been densely populated and heavily impacted for hundreds of years. Not surprisingly, these are often the areas of relatively low relief and without striking landscapes. Given the vulnerability of karst environments, extreme land and groundwater degradation has commonly occurred.

Careful management of the flow and condition of fluids (water and air) through cave systems is commonly critical to the successful management of caves. Further, safeguarding natural processes is fundamental to karst management. In turn, that implies the need for careful management of the vegetation and soils of entire water catchment areas. Directions of underground drainage in karst areas are typically dictated by geological structures and surface topography can give a quite misleading picture - indeed in well developed karst there may be no consistent surface drainage patterns. Dry valleys are common on the surface, and underground waters often breach surface drainage divides, sometimes flowing from one valley to another and often flowing uphill under pressure in confined solution channels.

Underground flow times are often rapid, opportunities for natural cleansing of polluted or sediment-laden groundwaters are largely lacking and pathogenic organisms can often survive the travel time. To such fundamental management concerns must be added engineering difficulties. These commonly include difficult foundation conditions for buildings and other structures, ground surface collapse and leaky artificial reservoirs.

Caves, often decorated by *speleothems,* such as stalactites and stalagmites, or even spectacular accumulations of ice in high altitude caves, are for most people the best-known elements of karst. They provide sites of beauty, mystery, excitement and challenge and thus, important resources for recreation and tourism.

There are now relatively few places where the opportunity exists to safeguard truly pristine karst. In addition to maintaining and preserving such sites, the focus must now be on correcting the negative results of past and present management, and on restoration ecology.

> *Their mysterious character and beauty has often caused attention to be focused specifically on caves and so diverted interest from the wider karst environment. Protection and management of this wider karst environment is important not only in its own right but also because it underpins the adequate protection of a cave or any other single element in a karst landscape.*

III. THE IMPORTANCE OF CAVES AND KARST

In addition to the importance of retaining examples of karst landforms and landscapes as part of a strategy to safeguard global geodiversity, a number of economic, cultural and scientific values may be present in karst areas. Hence, there may be a diversity of demands that are in conflict with one another.

ECONOMIC VALUES

Agriculture, forestry, water management, limestone extraction and tourism are usually the most important forms of economic activity in karst areas.

Most of the world's population is dependent upon agriculture, and agriculture is ultimately dependent upon the upper few centimetres of the Earth's surface. Some karsts offer rich and highly productive soils that are utilised for both general and specialised agriculture. Millions of people live in karst areas, but karst soils are often particularly vulnerable due to degradation by a variety of karst-specific processes that add to the usual pressures on soil. Caves are sometimes used for some specialised forms of agriculture and industry, including fish breeding, mushroom growing and cheese production. In South-east Asia, the natural occurrence of cave swiftlets provides a major industry in harvesting of nests and this appears at present to be ecologically sustainable. However, any such industry should be monitored to ensure that over-harvesting does not occur.

It is estimated that one quarter of the world's population gain their water supplies from karst, either from discrete springs or from karst groundwater. Thus in some karsts settlement patterns have been strongly influenced by sources of water. Ancient Mayan people made extensive use of caves and *cenotes*; more recently, major engineering works have been undertaken in the karsts of Slovenia and in China. Irrigation, hydro-electric energy and fisheries are other major uses to which karst waters are put. Water supply may be particularly difficult to obtain in karst areas upstream of major springs, whether for agriculture or for human consumption. Pollutants can be transported rapidly through subsurface networks.

In some karsts major forest resources exist, or have previously existed. However, drought stress exacerbated by free drainage can be a significant constraint on silviculture, and forest removal can sometimes cause irreversible soil loss and hydrological changes.

Limestone is an important resource with application in many areas of agriculture and industry, for example, as a flux in steel making, and it is also used to reduce some forms of industrial pollution, for example, removal of sulphur dioxide gases. Limestone extraction for building stone, agriculture or other industrial purposes is a common source of conflict with other karst users and values, and needs careful planning and execution. Important mineralisation has occurred in some karsts, and limestone terrain sometimes overlies sediments of interest to the oil industry.

Tourism is a major economic activity in some karsts, including the use of both developed and undeveloped caves, and surface scenery, thereby generating local employment. Every year around 20 million people visit tourist caves globally, while Mammoth Cave, Kentucky (USA) receives over 2 million visitors annually. There are some 650 tourist caves with lighting systems worldwide, not counting caves used for "wild" cave tours where visitors carry their own lights. Remote appreciation is also possible by means of films, videos and photographic volumes, the production of which can be a significant component of some local economies. Such media also reinforce the value of caves and karst for tourism and as environments which need caring for.

In some parts of the world caves are used as sanitoria for respiratory and other ailments, especially where hot springs are also present, as at Banff (Canada) and Budapest (Hungary). Some caves are still used for permanent residence. Others are used for shelter, and as sites of refuge from air raids or for military activities. The sustainability of such use often depends upon a good supply of clear air and water.

SCIENTIFIC VALUES

A wide variety of scientific values exists in karst environments.

In terms of the earth sciences, karsts offer bedrock geologists clear exposures of lithological units, geological structures and minerals, and offer palaeontologists access to important fossil sites. Geomorphologists derive insight into landform evolution and climate change over broad areas from the morphology of particular caves and the study of cave sediments. Caves often contain important archaeological and palaeontological material which is well preserved only in this environment.

To the life scientist, karst is important as a host for special or endangered plant and animal species and communities both at the surface and underground. Some karsts have served as refuges for species that have persisted underground through environmental changes which have eliminated their surface dwelling relatives. Bats are probably the creatures most commonly associated with caves, but a variety of often endemic vertebrate and invertebrate animals inhabit karst, some of which may have only small population numbers or be highly adapted to the constancy of the underground environment. In many, but not all karsts, environmental conditions underground can be very constant and cave species may have little tolerance to subsurface environmental change. Subfossil palaeontology is often also an important value.

This harvestman, Holonuncia sp., from Abercrombie Caves, Australia, is a typical cave-adapted species. (photo S. Eberhard)

HUMAN VALUES

Some karsts are important for spiritual, religious, aesthetic, recreational and educational reasons.

In many parts of the world societies attach considerable importance to certain caves and other limestone landforms, as in the case of Mayan use of caves as temples. Many Hindu and Buddhist societies have established underground temples in caves. Some Buddhist communities build temples that mimic caves, as with the great temple of Sokkurum in South Korea and temples built in Rangoon for the World Buddhist Conference. In some cases spiritual values relate to underground waters. Mayan priests prayed for assistance in water management to the water god Chac. Certain karst springs, such as those at Muktinath in Nepal, are sacred to both Buddhists and Hindus. For Christians too some caves are of considerable spiritual importance, such as the grotto at Lourdes. Few western tourist caves lack a "cathedral chamber", further emphasising the spiritual connections some feel with cave environments. Around the world caves continue to be used as burial sites, and places of worship continue to be erected amid karst, for example in the karst towers of Southern China and Malaysia.

Many of the world's most scenic environments owe much of their appeal to karstic phenomena, including many mountain areas that draw walkers, climbers, photographers, artists and nature lovers. Caving is a significant recreational activity in some parts of the world, while every year millions of people visit developed tourist caves.

The various economic, spiritual and scientific values of karst are often readily demonstrated in a compact area, and commonly make caves and karst areas splendid examples for education. In few environments are the ecological chains of cause and affect, and environmental determinants on human society, so clearly evident.

Cultural resource management is often an important consideration in karst areas. Some springs and caves have long served as foci for human settlement or activity and now contain valuable records of the evolution of societies layer by layer, in sediment or in art upon the cave walls. The prehistoric legacy found in some caves is well known and has contributed in a major way to knowledge of our ancestors. The historical archaeology of some karsts is also important, including such features as water reticulation systems established in some Chinese karsts.

Considerable heritage value is attached to the built environment in some karst areas, ranging from some prehistoric constructions in caves to some cave resorts in Europe and the distinctive cave-associated tourist hotels of Australia and the USA.

Guideline

1. Effective planning for karst regions demands a full appreciation of all their economic, scientific and human values, within the local cultural and political context.

IV. THREATS TO CAVES AND KARST

It is fundamentally important to recognise that the proper protection of caves and karst is not just a matter of preserving interesting, beautiful or scientifically interesting natural features. In most cases, protection has far-reaching environmental implications which in turn generate significant economic impacts. In particular proper management of karst is an essential element of water resources management.

Caves and karsts are especially vulnerable and probably more so than most other land resources. In the first place, the integrity of any karst system is dependent upon a specific kind of relationship between water, land, vegetation and soils; this water is often drawn from a wide catchment area; any disturbance in the hydrologic system will threaten the karst and those caves which have a continuing relationship to the water levels or water quality. At the same time, any damage to the integrity of a karst system will have far-reaching hydrologic impacts. It also needs to be recognised that groundwater divides and catchment boundaries may not coincide with surface divides.

Secondly, many other caves, left abandoned by the original formative waters as groundwater levels have been lowered, will be relatively dry, relatively static in character and essentially non-renewable. Most of the non-limestone caves, *e.g.*, volcanic caves, also fall into this latter grouping. However, dripwater flows and catchment hydrology remain significant to both the geochemical processes within caves and to cave biota, and more particularly through the influence which moisture exerts upon cave microclimates.

The distinction here between those caves with a continuing relationship to the water-table and those which have long been abandoned by the water and stand clear from it also highlights a further distinction. Those with active streams or seasonal flooding, are subject to high levels of kinetic energy which cause continuing change within the cave. These changes in turn often quickly eliminate the evidence of other lesser changes, such as those caused by entry of visitors. However, other caves may have extremely low energy throughputs; the major energy inputs may only be, for instance, the excreta of cave crickets and circadian air movements. In such a low energy system, the impact of human entry, no matter how carefully managed, may be considerable.

The entrance to Atea Kanada, Papua New Guinea. This is an example of a high energy cave system(river flow of 4 cubic metres/sec) and presents a major challenge to explorers, but the impact of human entry upon such a system is negligible. (photo D. Gillieson)

There is a continuum of threats from the very direct ones of physical change (*e.g.*, the total destruction of a cave by quarrying), to the indirect threats, where, for instance, the use of a cave for recreation results in gradual but unrelenting compaction of floors and so to extinction of cave fauna which depends upon uncompacted floors. Other indirect effects include the introduction of moulds and other contaminating organisms. Although it is difficult to set a clear boundary between these, we will endeavour below to deal with each topic in a sequence which reflects its place in such a continuum.

TOTAL DESTRUCTION

Caves or even major karst landscapes may be totally destroyed by mining, quarrying, by being bulldozed away for engineering works or other developments, by becoming submerged below artificial water storages, or filled in with waste or refuse. These issues are amongst the most obvious of threats, occur with increasing frequency, and often generate major conflicts over land use.

MAJOR LAND OR HYDROLOGIC DISTURBANCE

While not causing direct destruction, forestry, quarrying, land clearance, construction, agricultural activities, waste disposal or other land fill, and other developmental activities may disrupt karst systems. Changes in soil cover, siltation of waterways (even from activities far outside of the actual karst landscape), diversion of, or changes in, water flow, and changes in vegetation cover can all have major impacts. Excessive withdrawing of water from an aquifer may well result in lowering of the water level, sometimes with disastrous and expensive consequences. Extractive industries such as speleothem harvesting, guano mining, removal of sculptured rocks and *karren* for garden decoration, or bird's nest harvesting may also result in massive impacts, particularly upon ecosystems within caves.

Excessive extraction of water from deep aquifers has resulted in spectacular and expensive destructive impacts. In the South-eastern United States, China and South Africa in particular, major land collapses have destroyed houses and commercial or industrial buildings and often led to considerable loss of human life.

POLLUTION

The dumping or discharge of various substances within a karst catchment area often results in severe pollution. Sewage and domestic, farm or industrial wastes are all common problems. There is also a major risk in pollution by gaseous hydrocarbons from fuel storages or waste sites.

Such pollution, whether by water-soluble compounds, microbial transmission, siltation or simply by dumping of large-scale wastes, is destructive. Many examples of problems due to groundwater pollution have been documented amongst the earliest being the 1854 cholera epidemic in Britain. Such problems continue to the present day. The comparatively rapid transmission of groundwater flows in karst provides little opportunity for natural filtering or other purifying effects, and so problems such as disease transmission may arise much more readily than in other terrain. Even if the source of the pollution is located far outside the karst area itself it can still have devastating impacts.

HUMAN UTILISATION OF CAVES

There are a remarkable range of human uses of caves *per se*. These include military purposes (for storage, shelter, guerrilla tactics, proposed nuclear shelters, *etc.*), religious observance or monuments, sanitoria, burial, manufacturing, water storage, dwelling sites, mushroom farming, cheese-making, wine-making and storage, smuggling, various aspects of scientific research, tourism in a range of forms, concert auditoria, and recreation at a number of levels. Some of these uses are of cultural significance, often enduring over many centuries. These traditional uses raise the oft-cited paradox that yesterday's great art is today's graffiti; both involve people drawing upon cave walls but their location in time gives them totally different meanings. Similarly, a present day proposal to establish a cheese factory in a European cave would probably meet with significant opposition, but it is extremely doubtful whether anybody would seriously propose discontinuing cheese manufacture at the Roquefort Cave.

These uses result in a wide range of impacts:

- alteration of the physical structure of the cave
- alteration of water chemistry
- alteration of cave hydrology
- alteration of air movements and micro-climate
- introduction of artificial light
- compaction or liquefaction of floors
- erosion of or disturbance to cave sediments and their contents
- destruction of speleothems
- destruction of fauna
- introduction of alien organisms or materials (*e.g.*, concrete, climbing aids), pollutants, nutrients, animal species, algae & fungi
- surface impacts, *e.g.*, erosion, siltation, vegetation change

These impacts may be independent of each other, cumulative or synergistic. Further there are complex relationships between the number of visitors to a cave at any one time, the frequency of visits and the resulting impact.

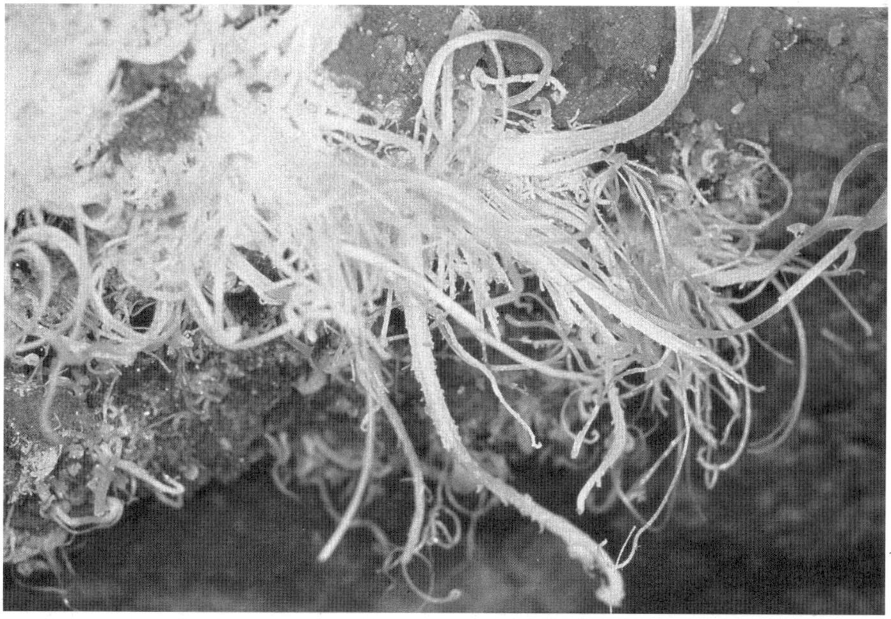

Halite speleothems in Mullamallang Cave, Nullarbor Plain, Australia. Delicate and beautiful decorations are generally only found in low energy caves and are particularly vulnerable. (photo E. Hamilton-Smith)

Caves and karst are amongst the most vulnerable of ecosystems, and are often subject to degradation as a result of phenomena or events which occur at a considerable distance. Their effective protection and management therefore requires consideration and action at both area and local levels.

The development of caves for tourism purposes may be done in a way which results minimal destructive impacts. The extent to which impacts occur may well be balanced by the opportunity for public education. However, the rush to profitability may lead to insensitive and damaging impacts, or may result in the development of too many such caves with the result that many are not financially viable and consequently abandoned allowing further damaging impacts to occur.

Guidelines

2. The integrity of any karst system depends upon an interactive relationship between land, water and air. Any interference with this relationship is likely to have undesirable impacts, and should be subjected to thorough environmental assessment.

3. Land managers should identify the total catchment area of any karst lands, and be sensitive to the potential impact of any activities within the catchment, even if not located on the karst itself.

4. Destructive actions in karst, such as quarrying or dam construction, should be located so as to minimise conflict with other resource or intrinsic values.
5. Pollution of groundwater poses special problems in karst and should always be minimised and monitored. This monitoring should be event-based rather than at merely regular intervals, as it is during storms and floods that most pollutants are transported through the karst system.
6. All other human uses of karst areas should be planned to minimise undesirable impacts, and monitored in order to provide information for future decision-making.
7. While recognising the non-renewable nature of many karst features, particularly within caves, good management demands that damaged features be restored as far as is practicable.
8. The development of caves for tourism purposes demands careful planning, including consideration of sustainability. Where appropriate, restoration of damaged caves should be undertaken, rather than opening new caves for tourism

V. SOME OPTIONS IN PROTECTION OF KARST

Mammoth Cave, Kentucky, USA, is protected as both a national park and a World Heritage Area. (photo G. Middleton)

Protection of karst features has all too often focused upon caves, and not given adequate consideration to the need for protection and proper management of the total karst area as a land unit.

Karst and caves may occur in, and be appropriately protected by, any one of the available categories of protected area (see Appendix 1). The category of protected area utilised for cave protection should be chosen to meet the protection needs of the site concerned.

Where a karst area as a whole, or any part of such an area, is under consideration, the protection strategy chosen should provide for protection of the total catchment wherever possible. Where this is not practicable, there should at least be an extensive buffer surrounding the key features to be protected. Where a significant part of the catchment lies outside of the protected area boundaries, then consideration should also be given to the use of environmental controls under planning or water management legislation to safeguard the quantity and quality of water inputs from these areas to the karst system.

It may also be possible to develop what is known in some countries as a *total catchment management* process, where all those responsible for the management of lands within a single catchment agree to adopt appropriate inter-related policies and programs to protect values within the catchment. Originally developed to protect water quality, this process has the potential to make an important contribution to management of karst or wetland areas.

At the other extreme, catchment issues may be less prominent in the protection of some karst phenomena such as an occurrence of an unusual form of karren or a specific biological habitat. In the unusual case of a single and perhaps isolated cave, standing clear of the water-table, it may be that adequate conservation might be achieved by natural monument protection. However, in all cases attention must be given to the safeguarding of groundwater catchments and local seepage.

Priority in protection should be given to areas or sites:

- having high natural, social or cultural value
- possessing a wide range of values within the one site
- which have suffered minimal environmental degradation
- of a type not well represented in the protected areas system of their country or biogeographic zone.

A special issue arises in relation to the protection of cave values. In a situation where there is long-established use of the surface land, but a major cave system below, it may not be necessary to change existing land-use if the cave can be protected in some other way.

The maintenance of natural flows of water and air must always be the first priority if the cave environment is to be maintained. More importantly, the long-term impacts of existing land-uses should be carefully assessed prior to any such decision and the legislative provision for this kind of protection should be fully integrated with other land protection legislation.

In Europe guidelines have also been developed for the selection of underground habitat protection based on specific biological criteria including the presence of rare or geographically restricted species and scientific values (Council of Europe, 1992). As indicated elsewhere, issues regarding the contents of caves, including biota, need to be examined in greater detail in a companion volume.

The possibility has often been raised of establishing an 'underground wilderness' area. These proposals essentially argue for declaration of an area which will only be entered (perhaps by a limited number) under minimum impact conditions, comparable with the restrictions placed upon existing wilderness areas on the surface. The concept may work effectively in a high energy cave system, but is problematic in any low energy system. Although protection of this kind has properly been instituted over a number of important caves in order to reduce the impact of entry, the term 'wilderness' may raise unrealistic expectations. While surface wilderness in many environments will have high regenerative capacities, the regenerative capacity of a low energy cave system is, within a human time scale, zero. Even minimal and sensitive entry will result in impacts, and these will generally be both irreversible and cumulative.

Special consideration needs to be given to the protection of karst areas which, for one reason or another, may legitimately not be included within protected areas. However, any actions or phenomena within these areas may well have impacts elsewhere. Such areas should be identified by public authorities, and, where necessary, planning controls or programs of public education might be introduced to ensure appropriate management. Consideration should also be given to heritage agreements or covenants approved by landowners and these should be appropriately recognised and rewarded by state land management policies.

The establishment of protected areas is not, in itself, enough to ensure karst protection. The management of karst demands specific interdisciplinary expertise and this is in the early stages of development in most countries. Management agencies should recognise the importance of this expertise and take advantage of inter-agency or international co-operation in order to enhance their own capacity.

Although legislative protection is vital, it is never enough in itself. Genuine protection must also be based in grass-roots support - and may even arise from and be based in grassroots initiatives. But this in turn demands a continuing program of active public education about resource protection.

Guidelines

9. Governments should ensure that a representative selection of karst sites is declared as protected areas (especially as category I - IV in Appendix 1) under legislation which provides secure tenure and active management.
10. Priority in protection should be given to areas or sites having high natural, social or cultural value; possessing a wide range of values within the one site; which have suffered minimal environmental degradation; and/or of a type not already represented in the protected areas system of their country.
11. Where possible, a protected area should include the total catchment area of the karst.
12. Where such coverage is not possible, environmental controls or total catchment management agreements under planning, water management or other legislation should be used to safeguard the quantity and quality of water inputs to the karst system.
13. Public authorities should identify karst areas not included within protected areas and give consideration to safeguarding the values of these areas by such means as planning controls, programs of public education, heritage agreements or covenants.
14. Management agencies should seek to develop their expertise and capacity for karst management.

VI. MANAGEMENT AT THE REGIONAL AND SITE LEVEL

Karst landforms, including caves, are the direct result of the operation of the solution process over long periods of geologic time. Nearly all of the karst solution process is moderated by factors operating on the surface of the karst and immediately below the surface. Surface vegetation regulates the flow of water into the underlying karst through interception, through the control of litter and roots on soil infiltration, and through the production of carbon dioxide, and hence carbonic acid, in the root zone. The metabolic uptake of water by plants, especially trees, may regulate the quantity of water available to supply cave decorations. Trees in particular are like large carbon dioxide pumps, releasing 20-25% of their atmospheric gas uptake through root respiration. Thus clear felling of forests, or major changes consequent on plantation establishment, may radically alter the flow and quality of water in the karst. Soil erosion in excess of the natural rates may infill streamsinks, dolines or joints. Changes to surface drainage resulting from contour banking, irrigation or river regulation may interrupt or drastically reduce the supply of karst water. The release of fertilisers, herbicides and insecticides from agricultural activities may compromise cave ecosystems beyond their capacity to recover. Water is the primary mechanism by which surface actions become subsurface impacts.

Karst management must be holistic in its approach and should aim to maintain the quality and quantity of water and air movement through the subterranean environment as well as the surface.

At the regional or site level, planning should be expressed through the development of management plans. These should be established by a process which involves and considers the interests of all stakeholders and should be open to public scrutiny and continuing or regular review. At the minimum, a management plan document should provide for :

- detailed delineation and description of the area
- a review of the key resources of the area and identification of threats or other issues in the management of these
- clarification of the desired outcomes (goals) in protection of the area concerned
- identification of principles and strategies in management of the area
- methods to be adopted in monitoring the effectiveness of the plan.

Guidelines

15. Managers of karst areas and specific cave sites should recognise that these landscapes are complex three-dimensional integrated natural systems comprised of rock, water, soil, vegetation and atmosphere elements.
16. Management in karst and caves should aim to maintain natural flows and cycles of air and water through the landscape in balance with prevailing climatic and biotic regimes.
17. Managers should recognise that in karst, surface actions may be sooner or later translated into impacts directly underground or further downstream.

In general, karst systems develop over geological timescales which must inevitably include significantly different environments from that of today. Some karst systems may be so changed due to prevailing conditions that they have no capacity to regenerate. Other systems may have some capacity to regenerate but this may entail timescales greater than that of individual human generations. Caves and their contents (speleothems, sediments and bones) may have been formed or emplaced under different climate regimes and may remain unaltered for millennia. These may require specific management attention because of their fragility.

Guidelines

18. Pre-eminent amongst karst processes is the cascade of carbon dioxide from low levels in the external atmosphere through greatly enhanced levels in the soil atmosphere to reduced levels in cave passages. Elevated soil carbon dioxide levels depend on plant root respiration, microbial activity and a healthy soil invertebrate fauna. This cascade must be maintained for the effective operation of karst solution processes.

19. The mechanism by which this is achieved is the interchange of air and water between surface and underground environments. Hence the management of quality and quantity of both air and water is the keystone of effective management at regional, local and site specific scales. Development on the surface must take into account the infiltration pathways of water.

> *The karst catchment boundary is not a single line that can be represented on a map, but a zone which has a dynamic outer boundary dependent on local details of surface geology and weather conditions.*

It is more useful to think of a core catchment area, within which flow will usually be directed to a particular cave network, and a peripheral or buffer catchment area which may be activated periodically. For the precautionary principle to apply in karst research or management, the larger catchment should be used to provide a truer representation of the sources for the karst drainage network. The catchment of a karst drainage system is usually much larger than just the area of limestone outcrop and the obvious non-karstic contributing catchment.

> *Defining the contributing catchment of a cave may be difficult and even, in some cases, impossible. The elucidation of the drainage network of Mammoth Cave, Kentucky USA, was the result of over twenty years' investigation and hundreds of dye tracing experiments.*

A minimalist approach would be to define the catchment as the area of limestone outcrop. This neglects the possibility that the limestone is continuous though not outcropping in a given terrain, or that surrounding non-karstic rocks are contributing significant quantities of water by surface or subsurface flow. In many cases a thick mantle of colluvium lies over the limestone and directly feeds cave systems. This is especially true in areas which were formerly glaciated or which have been subject to repeated mass movements over geologic time.

Subterranean breaches of surface drainage divides occur more frequently than is generally realised and the exact conditions for the activation of conduits may depend on storm events or previous rainfall. In some cases abandoned conduits may be re-activated. Thus the definition of a karst catchment is imprecise and must have a dynamic boundary to take account of extreme events. This is best achieved by constructing buffer zones around limestone regions, in which any change to land use must be preceded by investigations of the drainage network and its dynamics using repeated planned dye-tracing experiments. Under these circumstances

"One well-designed tracer test, properly done, and correctly interpreted, is worth 1000 expert opinions or 100 computer simulations of groundwater flow" (Quinlan, 1990).

Guideline

20. Catchment boundaries commonly extend beyond the limits of the rock units in which the karst has formed. The whole karst drainage network should be defined using planned water tracing experiments and cave mapping. It should be recognised that the boundary of these extended catchments can fluctuate dramatically according to weather conditions, and that relict cave passages can be reactivated following heavy rain.

For karst areas, the concept of total catchment management becomes vital. This involves the coordinated management and utilisation of physical resources of land, water and vegetation within the boundaries of a catchment to ensure sustainable use and to minimise land degradation. Proper environmental management of karst terrains rests on a base of public acceptance that clear linkages exist between surface and underground systems, and that these linkages are of fundamental importance to karst system function.

Guideline

21. More than in any other landscape, a total catchment management regime must be adopted in karst areas. Activities undertaken at specific sites may have wider ramifications in the catchment due to the ease of transfer of materials in karst.

There are numerous examples of accelerated soil erosion on karst areas worldwide. Limestone soils tend to be shallow and stony with low to moderate nutrient holding capacity because of excessive leaching due to free drainage. There is thus a strong tendency for devegetated or heavily used limestone soils to erode down to bedrock surfaces quite rapidly.

This soil stripping can be seen in the extreme bare glaciokarst of the Burren, Ireland; the classic Dinaric karst of Slovenia; the Guizhou polygonal karst of China; and the karst of Vancouver Island, B.C. The process was first noticed some 2000 years ago in Greece and continues today in many limestone areas. Eroded soil material is rapidly transferred underground to block passages, divert or impound cave streams, or smother cave life. Soil erosion control is therefore a high priority for karst managers, and much depends on the effectiveness of revegetation. In many karst areas naturally evolved native forests have been cleared and replaced with monospecific plantation forests, often coniferous. These plantations have higher basal area and often higher water demand per hectare than the forests they replace. Thus there may be a reduction in the flow of percolation water to the karst system, as well as some sediment transfer associated with felling and road construction. Caves underlying introduced coniferous forest have high root biomasses visible and are relatively dry. There is usually accelerated soil loss and tree decline associated with forestry operation on karst. On Vancouver Island, British Columbia, forests clearfelled since 1900 have only regained 17% of the original timber volume after 75 years, and soil depth loss ranges from a mean of 25% five years after logging to 60% after ten years. Clear guidelines for forestry operations on karst need to be developed and adhered to.

Guidelines

22. Soil management must aim to minimise erosive loss and alteration of soil properties such as aeration, aggregate stability, organic matter content and a healthy soil biota.

23. A stable natural vegetation cover should be maintained as this is pivotal to the prevention of erosion and maintenance of critical soil properties.

Karst waters can be viewed as types of wild rivers where the drainage network is not as obvious as in surface streams, and there is complexity in hydrological linkages and in flow regimes. In many mountain areas the highest parts of karst catchments are still forested and inaccessible. In such areas both water quantity and quality are maintained along with the integrity of ecosystems.

The maintenance of water quality in karst can be viewed as a common good which is becoming increasingly important in those areas where rural populations are increasing rapidly and the settlement of karst is well established.

In areas such as China and the Philippines recent new settlement of karst terrain is creating challenges for sustainable management of karst resources, especially water and soil.

Guideline

24. Establishment and maintenance of karst protected areas can contribute to the protection of both the quality and quantity of groundwater resources for human use. Catchment protection is necessary both on the karst and on contributing non-karst areas. Activities within caves may have detrimental effects on regional groundwater quality.

Pollutants readily enter karst drainage systems and are rapidly transmitted through cave conduits. The range of likely pollutants includes nitrates and phosphates, chlorides, heavy metals, hydrocarbons, industrial acids, bacteria and viruses.

There is a great potential for hydrologic change within developed karst tourism sites due to the construction of pathways, entrance structures, car parks and toilets. Above a cave, the surfacing of the land with concrete or bitumen renders it nearly impermeable, in contrast to the high natural porosity of karst. Thus the feedwater for stalactites may be drastically reduced or eliminated. Drains may alter flow patterns and deliver additional percolating water to certain areas of a cave, causing changes in speleothem deposition. One way to minimise these effects if development above caves cannot be avoided is to use gravel surfaced car parks or to include infiltration strips and cross drains in the car park design. Similarly, pathways may need to be hardened for foot traffic, but this should be permeable (gravel, raised walkways, pavers) rather than concrete or bitumen. Toilet facilities may leak into karst fissures or conduits. There are many tourist sites where sewage reticulation or septic tank systems have leaked or overflowed into caves. There is a welcome trend to use either pump-out toilet systems, where wastes are dispersed as sprays or sludges away from the karst, or composting toilets where residues are dehydrated and may be subsequently used as fertiliser.

Guideline

25. Management should aim to maintain the natural transfer rates and quality of fluids, including gases, through the integrated network of cracks, fissures and caves in the karst. The nature of materials introduced must be carefully considered to avoid adverse impacts on air and water quality.

Limestone, dolomite, magnesite and marble are quarried world-wide and used for cement manufacture, as an aggregate, as high grade building stone, for agricultural lime, for abrasives and for many other uses. Most resource conflict over limestone mining revolves around visual and water pollution, as well as loss of recreational and conservation values. Limestone bodies with high relief which are ideal for mining are often the most cavernous, and there is often conflict and compromise when there is a high expectation of continued access to this resource as well as a strong conservation movement.

This recent example of quarry restoration in progress at Ida Bay, Tasmania, shows the attention being given to maintaining water quality. (photo D. Gillieson)

Guideline

26. The extraction of rocks, soil, vegetation and water will clearly interrupt the processes that produce and maintain karst, and therefore such uses must be carefully planned and executed to minimise environmental impact. Even the apparently minor activity of removing limestone pavement or other karren for ornamental decoration of gardens or buildings has a drastic impact and should be subject to the same controls as any major extractive industry.

Fire management on limestone areas is a contentious subject, especially when severe wildfires have previously caused loss of life or property. In many societies fire is widely used as a vegetation clearance tool. Most karsts have a low natural fire frequency due to the shielding effects of limestone outcrops, reduced ground cover and often a more dense canopy with rainforest elements in the flora. In some karsts of eastern Australia, natural fire frequencies are poorly documented but the fire interval may be 35 to 50 years or greater. Under these conditions relict vegetation types may survive, for example the dry monsoon rainforests of north Queensland. In these karsts sediment transport only occurs immediately after fires, with minimal soil erosion in the intervening periods.

Hazard reduction burning is widely used by land managers, but may have deleterious effects on karst areas.

In Australia for example many authorities aim to burn individual areas on a five to seven year cycle. This increased frequency reduces the fuel load but often promotes more fire tolerant vegetation, or changes the vegetation understorey. Thus there is potential for changes to the hydrology of the underlying karst particularly if highly organic surface soils or peat are burned. Although there may be a management prescription to avoid burning limestone outcrops, unplanned escape of fires into sensitive areas occurs due to weather changes. Increased stream siltation and cave sedimentation may result. A careful zoning of fire management, aided by mapping of past fire boundaries with buffers around karst areas, may help to reduce these impacts. Historical fire records using mapped data and oral histories are another valuable resource in this regard. The study of fire histories using sedimentary charcoal in caves is a promising avenue for research.

Guideline

27. Imposed fire regimes on karst should, as far as is practicable, mimic those occurring naturally.

Human visiting of caves may have a significant cumulative impact upon physical and biological values at both the site level and regional level (Spate and Hamilton-Smith, 1991). There is therefore a need to prepare and implement management plans that provide access to caves, ensure appropriate limits on visitor numbers where necessary, and institute both minimal impact visitor practices and suitable tracks or other means to protect the environment. Time scales for revegetation are extremely long compared with other systems; or it may, in practice, be impossible.

Speleologists entering this highly decorated section of a cave in Western Australia must remove their boots and protective overalls and also remain on narrow pathways marked by transparent plastic sheeting on the floor. (photo J. Watson)

There is considerable merit in the formulation of a "minimal impact code" for cave visitors, including scientists engaged in research. Such a code can be promulgated through visitor information services in protected areas, through youth groups and speleological organisations and through permit conditions. These practices are generally intended to apply in caves where visitors are likely to have a detrimental impact on the cave simply by entering the cave. The basic principles of formulating such a code are as follows:

- a minimal impact code based on consensus amongst user groups and managers is more likely to be successful than rules imposed by a management authority.
- responsible actions serve as a better example to others than authoritarian instructions.
- the systematic documentation, mapping and publication of data about caves (excepting entrance locations) is a responsibility of all users of the cave environment, and should be encouraged by management authorities.
- the best natural protection for caves and karst is the increase in self-awareness of individual visitors, especially with respect to their environmental impact and responsibilities.

- every cave visit or caving trip has an impact. Leaders of caving teams and management authorities should ask if a trip into a particular cave is necessary, and if is there another cave, less vulnerable to damage, that can be visited.

Useful codes have been developed in several countries including Australia, the UK and Switzerland. An extract of the Australian code is given in Table 1.

Table 1: Minimal Impact Caving Code, 1995 - Australian Speleological Federation (Inc)

1. Remember EVERY caving trip has an impact. Is this trip into this cave necessary? If it is just for recreation, is there another cave that is less vulnerable to damage that can be visited? Make this assessment depending on the purpose of your visit, the size and experience of the proposed party, and IF THE TRIP IS LIKELY to damage the cave.
2. Where possible the party leader should have visited the cave previously and hence should be aware of sensitive features of the cave, the best anchor points, and generally reduce the need for unnecessary exploration.
3. Cave slowly. You will see and enjoy more, and there will be less chance of damage to the cave and to yourself. This especially applies when you are tired and exiting a cave.
4. If there are beginners on a trip, make sure that they are close to an experienced caver, so that the experienced caver can help them when required, e.g. in difficult sections. Ensure that the party caves at the pace of the slowest caver.
5. Keep your party size small - 4 is a good party size.
6. Cave as a team - help each other through the cave. Don't split up unless impact is reduced by doing so.
7. Constantly watch your head placement AND that of your party members. Let them know before they are likely to do any damage.
8. Keep caving packs as small as possible or don't use them in sensitive caves or extensions.
9. Ensure that party members don't wander about the cave unnecessarily.
10. Stay on all marked or obvious paths. If no paths are marked or none is obvious - define ONE!
11. Learn to recognise cave deposits or features that may be damaged by walking or crawling on them.
12. Take care in the placement of hands and feet throughout a cave.

13. Wash your caving overalls and boots regularly so that the spread of bacteria and fungi are minimised.
14. If a site is obviously being degraded examine the site carefully to determine if an alternative route is possible. Any alternative route MUST not cause the same or greater degradation than the currently used route. If an alternative is available suggest the alternative route to the appropriate management authority and report the degradation.
15. Carry in-cave marking materials while caving and restore any missing markers. Tape off sensitive areas you believe are being damaged and report the damage to the appropriate management authority.
16. If it is necessary to walk on flowstone in a cave remove any muddied boots and or clothing before proceeding OR DON'T PROCEED! Sometimes it is better to assess the situation and return at a later date with the appropriate equipment.
17. Treat the cave biota with respect, watch out for them, and avoid damaging them and their "traps", webs, etc. Also avoid directly lighting cave biota if possible.
18. If bone material is found on existing or proposed tracks it should be moved off the track to a safer location if at all possible. Collection should only be undertaken with appropriate permission.
19. If you eat food in a cave ensure that small food fragments are not dropped as this may impact the cave biota. One way is to carry a plastic bag to eat over and catch the food fragments. This can then be folded up and removed from the cave.
20. Ensure that all foreign matter is removed from caves. This includes human waste. If long trips are to be made into a cave ensure that containers for the removal of liquid and solid waste are included on the trip inventory.
21. When rigging caves with artificial anchors, e.g. traces, tapes, rope etc, ensure that minimal damage occurs to the anchor site by protecting the site. For example protect frequently used anchors, e.g. trees, with carpet, packs, cloth, etc. Bolts should only be used where natural anchors are inappropriate.
22. CAVE SOFTLY!

Guideline

28. While it is desirable that people should be able to visit and appreciate karst features such as caves, the significance and vulnerability of many such features means that great care must be taken to minimise damage, particularly when cumulative over time. Management planning should recognise this fact and management controls should seek to match the visitor population to the nature of the resource.

VII. INTERNATIONAL CO-OPERATION AND LIAISON

There is a range of levels at which international co-operation and liaison may be of considerable assistance:

INFORMATION EXCHANGE, TECHNICAL ADVICE AND TRAINING

At the simplest, exchange of information may well further the work of those involved with protection of natural resources. This may take place through exchange of publications, use of electronic media, meeting at conferences or seminars, study visits, and doubtless many other means. This set of guidelines is in itself an example, having been developed for this purpose by the Working Group on Cave and Karst Protection of the IUCN World Commission on Protected Areas.

The International Union of Speleology, with its membership network of national speleological organisations, can and does play a particularly important role in fostering such exchange. In particular it provides a forum which brings together both professional scientists and recreational cave explorers and surveyors. Its *Speleological Abstracts (Bulletin Bibliographique Spéléologique)* provides a continually improving access to world literature. Further, its documentation commission is developing comparable protocols for cave and karst databases, making extensive use of electronic media in doing so.

Other scientific organisations, such as the International Geographic Union, foster and integrate scientific understanding of karst and caves. They also play a fundamentally important role in information exchange. The International Show Caves Association and the newly established International Subterranean Heritage Association will also make a valuable contribution, particularly as resources for public education.

The development of expertise within management agencies and the establishment of national or regional bodies, such as the American Cave Conservation Association and the Australasian Cave & Karst Management Association, centrally concerned with cave and karst management or conservation, are also providing important opportunities to integrate knowledge and understanding as a basis for further dissemination of expertise through information exchange.

British and Australian speleologists assist in providing a training seminar for National Park managers in Thailand. (photo E. Hamilton-Smith)

Those with specialised knowledge and experience in cave and karst protection may well undertake advisory, consultancy or training roles in furthering the protection of cave and karst areas. The various organisations already referred to above provide an avenue for the identification of appropriate expertise.

There are a number of ways in which technical expertise might be utilised. Management authorities can be assisted to:

- identify sites in need of protection and delineate appropriate boundaries for such sites.
- develop total catchment management or similar co-operative processes.
- develop appropriate processes for management planning and produce management plans.
- develop specific strategies, *eg.*, water quality, fire management or visitor management programs.
- generate environmentally sound development plans for caves or other tourism attractions in karst areas.
- train and develop staff skills in karst management.

JOINT ACTION

Two or more authorities or even countries may well collaborate to share responsibility in protection and management. One well-known example involves the Aggtelek karst of central Europe, where close co-operation between two national governments has provided for protection and management of an outstanding karst resource. Such an arrangement provides for coordinated management of a specific resource and for compatible strategies to be adopted which span national or other boundaries.

On a smaller but much more widespread basis, responsibility for a karst catchment is often divided between two or more different management tenures. The development of total catchment management policies and programs on a cooperative basis is vital for adequate protection of the resource in these situations.

At another level, the establishment of inter-agency partnerships (perhaps best practice partnerships - a growing trend in park management) can further the capacity of all parties.

POLICY DEVELOPMENT

One of the areas in which international information exchange is important is the development of protected area policies. Although these are often generalised and do not deal specifically with particular kinds of resource, *e.g.*, karst, an increasing number of management agencies do have documented karst management policies. There may also be well-recognised policies and practices in place which have not been made explicit in any formal document.

The documentation of cave and karst protection/management policies should be encouraged, and such policies made widely available to other management authorities.

PROTECTED AREAS INFORMATION

Although many cave and karst areas have been included in protected areas (*e.g.*, in the UK, the USA, Australia, New Zealand, Thailand, Malaysia, Japan), there is no systematic documentation of which areas are protected in this way.

There is also a need to identify major unprotected areas which deserve recognition and to assess the degree of protection given to all sites. An appropriate data base, perhaps at the World Conservation Monitoring Centre, should be established at an early date.

WORLD HERITAGE CONVENTION

A number of cave and karst sites have been recognised under the World Heritage Convention (*e.g.*, Mammoth-Flint Ridge system, Skocjanske Jama, Castleguard Cave, the Aggtelek karst, Carlsbad Caverns and Naracoorte Caves).

A review of existing recognised sites should be undertaken in order to (a) clarify the application of the heritage criteria to karst sites, and (b) identify high-value sites not yet included so that the respective governments might be encouraged to nominate them.

> *International co-operation can play a vital role in strengthening the karst management capacity of land management agencies and in ensuring integrated protection on a world basis.*

Guidelines

29. International, regional and national organisations concerned with aspects of karst protection and management should recognise the importance of international co-operation and do what they can to disseminate and share expertise.
30. The documentation of cave and karst protection/management policies should be encouraged, and such policies made widely available to other management authorities.
31. Data bases should be prepared listing cave and karst areas included within protected areas, but also identifying major unprotected areas which deserve recognition. Karst values of existing and potential World Heritage sites should be similarly recorded.

VIII. EPILOGUE

Karst and caves are very special and unique places, and yet highly dependent upon wider influences over which protected area managers may have very limited control.

It must be stressed once more that the guidelines presented above must always be applied in a *local* context. This will include recognition of local biodiversity and geodiversity, plus sensitivity towards socio-economic and political factors.

Hopefully the guidelines will provide managers and planners with useful aids towards improving community awareness of karst and cave systems, and hence increase the opportunity to secure local acceptance of and involvement in improved protection and management. The guidelines should also assist in preparation of more specific strategies or management plans at a national, regional or site level.

This volume is a first attempt to bring together as many key issues as possible relating to karst and cave protection in a relatively small booklet. Hopefully it will be widely distributed and widely used.

Constructive criticism is **earnestly** sought so that upon future revision it can improve its usefulness towards karst and cave protection. Meanwhile, the WCPA Working Group on Cave and Karst Protection will continue to provide advice to the best of its ability, if only to direct requests for help to known sources of special expertise. We welcome your ongoing interest and support.

IX. REFERENCES AND FURTHER READING

There is an absolutely voluminous literature on caves, karst and cave exploration. We have listed below a few 'benchmark' references only. Access to extensive bibliographies may be obtained through the organisations listed in Appendix 2.

Bogli, A. (1980). *Karst hydrology and physical speleology*, Berlin, Springer.

Camacho, Ana Isabel (1992). *The Natural History of Biospeleology*, Madrid, Museo Nacional de Ciencias Naturales.

Chapman, P. (1993). *Caves and Cave Life*, London, Harper Collins.

Council of Europe (1992). *Convention on the Conservation of European Wildlife and Natural Habitats, Standing Committee Recommendation No 36 on the conservation of underground habitats*, 154-156.

Courbon, P. & Chabert, C. (1979). *Atlas des Grands Gouffres du Monde*, Marseille, Editions J. Lafitte.

Courbon, P. Chabert, C., Bosted, P. & Lindsley, K. (1989). *Atlas of the Great Caves of the World.* St. Louis, Cave Books.

European Commission (1995). COST action 65. *Hydrogeological aspects of groundwater protection in karstic areas.* Directorate-General XII Science, Research and Development. Luxembourg / Brussels.

Fenton, M. B. (1983). *Just Bats*, Toronto, University of Toronto Press

Ford, D. C. & Williams, P. W. (1989). *Karst Geomorphology and Hydrology* London, Unwin Hyman Ltd, 601pp.

Gillieson, D. (1996). *Caves: Processes, Development and Management*, Oxford, Blackwell Publishers, 324pp.

Jennings, J. N. (1985). *Karst Geomorphology*, Oxford, Basil Blackwell Ltd, 293pp.

Kiernan, Kevin (1988). *The Management of Soluble Rock Landscapes : An Australian Perspective.* Sydney : Speleological Research Council Ltd.

Lowe, D. & Waltham, T. (1995). *A Dictionary of Karst and Caves.* London : British Cave Research Association.

Maire, R. (1981). *Synthese hydrogeologique et karstologique*, Spelunca Suppl. 3, 23-30.

Marie, R. (1990). La haute montaigne calcaire. *Karstologia Mémoires* 3, 731pp.

Quinlan, J. (1990). Special problems of ground-water monitoring in karst terrains, In Nielsen, D. M. and Johnson, A. I. (Eds), *Ground Water and Vadose Zone Monitoring*, ASTM, STP 1053, pp275 - 304.

Spate, A. & Hamilton-Smith, E. (1991). Cavers' impacts - some theoretical and applied considerations. In Bell, P., (Ed). *Proceedings of the Ninth ACKMA Conference, Margaret River, Western Australia, September 1991,* Australasian Cave and Karst Management Association.

Stebbings, R. E. (1988). *Conservation of European Bats*, London, Christopher Helm.

Trudgill, S. (1985). *Limestone Geomorphology*, London, Longmans.

White, W. B. (1988). *Geomorphology and hydrology of carbonate terrains*, Oxford, Oxford University Press.

APPENDIX 1

IUCN Categories and management objectives of protected areas (1996)

I. Strict Nature Reserve/Wilderness Area: protected area managed mainly for science or wilderness protection.

To protect nature and maintain natural processes in an undisturbed state in order to have ecologically representative examples of the natural environment available for appreciation, scientific study, environmental monitoring, education, and for the maintenance of genetic resources in a dynamic and evolutionary state.

II. National Park: protected area managed mainly for ecosystem protection and recreation.

To protect outstanding natural and scenic areas of national or international significance for scientific, educational, and recreational use. These are relatively large natural areas not materially altered by human activity where extractive uses are not allowed.

III. Natural Monument: protected area managed mainly for conservation of specific natural features.

To protect and preserve nationally significant natural features because of their special interest or unique characteristics. These are relatively small areas focused on protection of specific features.

IV. Habitat/Species Management Area: protected area managed mainly for conservation through management intervention.

To assure the natural conditions necessary to protect nationally significant species, groups of species, biotic communities, or physical features of the environment where these may require specific human manipulation for their perpetuation.

V. Protected Landscapes and Seascapes: protected areas managed mainly for landscape/seascape conservation and recreation.

To maintain nationally significant natural landscapes which are characteristic of the harmonious interaction of humans and land while providing opportunities for public enjoyment through recreation and tourism within the normal life style and economic activity of these areas. These are mixed cultural/natural landscapes of high scenic value where traditional land uses are maintained.

VI. Managed Resource Protected Area: protected area managed mainly for the sustainable use of natural ecosystems.

To protect the natural resources of the area for future use and prevent or contain development activities that are not sustainable.

Note: World Heritage sites (natural) and Biosphere Reserves are not listed as categories in their own right but are international designations recorded nationally under one of the above categories of protected area.

APPENDIX 2

WCPA Working Group on Cave and Karst Protection

The WCPA Working Group on Cave and Karst Protection includes cave managers, speleologists, administrators, researchers and protected area managers from throughout the world who share a common concern for the future of caves and karst resources and who support the following:

1. Caves, associated underground systems, surface karst, are important components of the earth with widespread global distribution.
2. Such areas are specially valuable for conservation, scientific research (biological, geological and anthropological), religious and spiritual purposes, recreation and tourism.
3. Such areas are particularly vulnerable to damage and pollution and therefore require careful protection and sensitive management, including surface catchment areas.
4. The considerable body of expert knowledge on cave and karst management within national and international speleological societies needs to be better known and applied by protected area management agencies.

A primary aim of the Working Group is to prepare and update as necessary guidelines on cave/karst protection.

Involvement in the Working Group is on a purely voluntary basis and the group has no formal operating budget. The Working Group welcomes new contributors who can help with its aims either directly of indirectly.

Enquiries and further information may be obtained from

Elery Hamilton-Smith,
WCPA Working Group on Cave and Karst Protection,
PO Box 36,
Carlton South,
Victoria 3053,
Australia.

Fax No: 61 3 9489 7785

Tel No: 61 3 9481 2439

E-mail : elery@melb.alexia.net.au

'Membership' as at April 1997

Note: Some of the addresses listed below may be outdated - if you experience any difficulty, please contact the Working Group convener. Furthermore, many members are available by fax and/or via E-mail.

German I. Andrade
Instituto para la Investigacion de
Recursos Biologicos
Alexander von Humboldt
Apartado Aereo 101447
Bogota
COLUMBIA

Philippe Axell
8 Chemin de la Vigne,
B-5580 BELVAUX
BELGIUM

Eugenio de Bellard Pietri
Apartado 802.10
Prados del Este
Caracas
VENEZUELA 080-A

Mihai Botez
Piata 14 Iulie, nr. 4
3400 Cluj Napoca
ROMANIA

Carlo Custodio
Protected Areas and Wildlife Bureau
Quezon Ave
Quezon City
PHILIPPINES

David Drew
Irish Speleological Union
Geography Dept
Trinity College
Dublin
IRELAND

Ofelia Espayos
Protected Areas and Wildlife Bureau
Quezon Ave
Quezon City
PHILIPPINES

Dr. Brian Finlayson
Dept of Geography
University of Melbourne
Parkville
Vict. 3052

Dr. David Gillieson
Dept of Geography & Ocenography
Australian Defence Force Academy
University of N.S.W.
Campbell
A.C.T. 2600

Paul Griffiths
P.O. Box 733
Gold River
British Columbia V0P 1G0
CANADA

Dr. John Gunn
Department of Geographical &
Environmental Sciences
University of Huddersfield
Queensgate
Huddersfield HD1 3DH
UNITED KINGDOM

Dr. Bill Halliday
6530 Cornwall Court
Nashville
TN 37205
U.S.A.

Elery Hamilton-Smith
P.O. Box 36
Carlton South
Vict. 3053

Paul Hardwick
Department of Geographical &
Environmental Sciences
University of Huddersfield
Queensgate
Huddersfield HD1 3DH
UNITED KINGDOM

Ian Houshold
Dept of Parks Wildlife & Heritage
P.O. Box 44A
Hobart
Tas.7001.

Prof. George Huppert
Dept of Geography
University of Wisconsin - La Crosse
La Crosse
Wisconsin 54601
U.S.A.

David Insall
Directorate-General of Nature
Protectorates
P.O. Box 461
Ruwi 112
SULTANATE OF OMAN

Dr. Julia James
School of Chemistry
University of Sydney
Sydney
N.S.W. 2006

Kevin Kiernan
15 Summerleas Rd
Fern Tree
Tas. 7054

Andre Kranjc
Karst Research Institute
Titov trg. 2, p.p.59
Sl-66230 Postojna
SLOVENIA

Olivier Langrand
WWF
BP 738
Antanarivo 101
MADAGASCAR

John E. Lattke
Dept of Entomology
University of California
Davis
CA 95616
U.S.A.

Sr. Clayton Perrieria Lino
Sociedad Braziliero de Espeleologia
Rua Joao Juliao, 296/11A
01323-020 Sao Paulo
BRAZIL

Marlynn M. Mendoza
Protected Areas and Wildlife Bureau
Quezon Ave
Quezon City
PHILIPPINES

David Meyers
Project Montagne D'Ambre, WWF
BP 294
Antanarivo 201
MADAGASCAR

Greg Middleton
Dept. Parks Heritage and Wildlife
P.O. Box 44A
Hobart
Tas. 7001

Susan Otuokon
Jamaica Conservation & Development
Trust
95 Dumbarton Ave
Kingston 10
JAMAICA

Phillip Parker
Council of Northern Caving Clubs
11 Manston Gardens
Crossgates
Leeds LS15 8EY
UNITED KINGDOM

Graham Price
National Caving Association
3 The Acorns
Oakhill
Bath
Somerset BA3 5BT
UNITED KINGDOM

Ivan Rubesa
Escuela de Geologia
Universidad Central de Venezuela
P.O. Box 60037
Caracas 1060-A
VENEZUELA

Peter Skoberne / Mario Simic
Zavod Republik Slovenije Za Varstvo
Naravne in Kulturne Dediscine
Plecnikov Trg 2
38661 Ljubljana
SLOVENIA

Dean Smart
Office of Natural Resources
Conservation
Royal Forest Department
Phahonyothin Rd
Bangkok 10900
THAILAND

Andy Spate
P.O. Box 452,
Queanbeyan,
N.S.W. 2620

Rob Stitt
1417 9th Ave
Seattle
WA 98119-3224
U.S.A.

Emma de la Vega Ricardo
Bellavista Np. 211 E/Julio S
Y Gonzalo de Q Reparto
Vigia
Camaguey - 2 CP 70200
CUBA

Dr. John Watson
CALM
44 Serpentine Rd
Albany
W.A. 6285

Rauleigh Webb
27 Beckenham St.
Beckenham
W. Aust. 6107

Nicholas White
123 Manningham St
West Parkville
Vict. 3052

Kevan Wilde
179 Crawford St.
St. Albans
Christchurch
N.Z.

Wang Xianpu
Institute of Botany
Chinese Academy of Sciences
CHINA

Charles Yonge
C/- EIUDP
Box 1357
Manado
Sulawesi Utam
INDONESIA

WCPA Personnel

Dr. Laurence Hamilton
342 Bittersweet Lane
Charlotte
VT 05445
U.S.A.

Adrian Phillips
2 The Old Rectory
Dumbleton
Near Evesham WR11 6TG
UNITED KINGDOM

David Sheppard
IUCN
Rue Mauverney 28
1996 Gland
SWITZERLAND

Lee Thomas
Environment Australia Biodiversity
Group
P.O. Box 636
Canberra
A.C.T. 2601

Jim Thorsell
IUCN
Rue Mauverney 28
1996 Gland
SWITZERLAND

IUCN Contacts

Adrian Phillips,
Chairman WCPA,

David Sheppard,
Protected Areas Programme,

Jim Thorsell,
Natural Heritage Programme,

IUCN,
Rue Mauverney 28,
CH 1196,
Gland,
Switzerland.

Other Useful Contacts

International Union of Spclcology
Dr Pavel Bosak, Secretary
Kalisnicka 4
CZ-13000 Praha 4
Czech Republic
Tel: 42 2 765 1444
Fax: 42 2 27 2460

International Subterranean Heritage
Association,
94 rue de la Culee,
B-6927 Resteigne,
Belgium.
Fax: 32 84 38 82 32
E-mail: isha@microresearch.be

International Show Caves Association
Largo Leone, 12
I-60040 Genga, Ancona
Italy

International Geographical Union
see John Gunn above

Electronic Information Sources

Many members of the Working Group may be contacted *via* E-mail through the convener.

There are also several useful sites on the Internet which provide access to a wide range of information on cave and karst issues:

http://alfred.uib.no/People/nglbn/index.htm
Romanian Speleology Home Page

http://fadr.msu.ru/caves/homepage.html
Speleo page of the Moscow State University

http://heureka.inf.elte.hu/barlang/
Hungarian Speleology Home Page

http://huizen.dds.nl/~mol/
GSG Home Page - Belgian Caving Club

http://mickey.iafrica.com/~peters/sasa/sasahome.html
South African Speleological Association (CapeSection)

http://net.onion.it:80/speleoit/caveit.html
Speleologia Italiana

http://rubens.its.unimelb.edu.au/~pgm/ackma/
Australasian Cave & Karst Management Association

http://rubens.its.unimelb.edu.au/~pgm/asf/
Australian Speleological Federation

http://rubens.its.unimelb.edu.au/~pgm/uis/
International Union of Speleology

http://rubens.its.unimelb.edu.au/~pgm/uisic/
UIS Informatics Commission

http://speleology.u.washington.edu/cavers/
Speleology Information Server USA

http://www.arpnet.it/~gspele/
Gruppo Speleologico Piemontese

http://www.camosun.bc.ca/~colesr/karstlnk.htm
Canadian & International Karst Resource and Conservation Links

http://www.caves.org/~nss/
The National Speleological Society USA

http://www.chebucto.ns.ca/~an388/cave.html
WWW Biospeleology Server

http://www.halcyon.com/samara/nssccms/welcome.html
Cave Conservation and Management Section NSS

http://www.ijs.si/slo-karst.html
Slovenian Karst

http://www.inria.fr/agos-sophia/sis/DB/database.html
World Cave Database

http://www.inria.fr/agos-sophia/sis/sis.html
Speleo INRIA Sophia

http://www.insa-lyon.fr/Labos/CASM/EFS/
Ecole Francaise de Speleologie

http://www.lrz-muenchen.de/u/uh101ad/www/cave/server.html
The Munich Speleo Server

http://www.microresearch.be/isha/
ISHA/AIPS Web Site

http://www.sat.dundee.ac.uk/~arb/bcra/
British Cave Research Association

http://www.sat.dundee.ac.uk/~arb/speleo.html
Andrew Brook's Server of Yorkshire and Scotland

http://www.tuke.sk/users/kladiva/doc/caveserverhp.html
Slovakia Cave Server

http://www.ul.ie/~sui/
Speleological Union of Ireland

http://www.wku.edu/www/geoweb/karst/
Center for Cave and Karst Studies Kentucky

http://www3.waikato.ac.nz/waitomo/
Waitomo Caves - New Zealand

APPENDIX 3

Glossary

Cenote A type of steep-walled collape doline that extends below the water table so as to contain a pool or lake.

Circadian A biological or behavioural process that recurs in an innate rhythm such as the daily cycle of sleep and wakedness in humans.

Doline A closed surface depression formed by karst processes, normally with internal drainage into a cave system or through bedrock fissures.

Duricrust A hard silica enriched soil horizon which commonly occurs in semi-arid landscapes and which often remains after erosion of overlying less hardened material.

Endemic Being only found in a certain locality; not naturally found elsewhere.

Karren Small scale sculpturing developed on limestone surfaces, either exposed to the rain or buried beneath the soil.

Karst A distinctive style or terrain that is characterised by individual landform types and landform assemblages that are largely the product of rock material having been dissolved by natural waters to a greater degree than in most landscapes.

Pseudokarst Terrain with landforms which resemble those of karst but which are not the product of karst (primarily solution) processes.

Speleologist An expert in the scientific study of caves.

Speleothem Decorations or deposits in caves caused by the re-crystallisation of dissolved minerals.

Stalagmite A calcite deposit growing up from a cave floor.

Stalactite A calcite deposit growing down from a cave roof.

APPENDIX 4

Guidelines (English)

1. Effective planning for karst regions demands a full appreciation of all their economic, scientific and human values, within the local cultural and political context.

2. The integrity of any karst system depends upon an interactive relationship between land, water and air. Any interference with this relationship is likely to have undesirable impacts, and should be subjected to thorough environmental assessment.

3. Land managers should identify the total catchment area of any karst lands, and be sensitive to the potential impact of any activities within the catchment, even if not located on the karst itself.

4. Destructive actions in karst, such as quarrying or dam construction, should be located so as to minimise conflict with other resource or intrinsic values.

5. Pollution of groundwater poses special problems in karst and should always be minimised and monitored. This monitoring should be event-based rather than at merely regular intervals, as it is during storms and floods that most pollutants are transported through the karst system.

6. All other human uses of karst areas should be planned to minimise undesirable impacts, and monitored in order to provide information for future decision-making.

7. While recognising the non-renewable nature of many karst features, particularly within caves, good management demands that damaged features be restored as far as is practicable.

8. The development of caves for tourism purposes demands careful planning, including consideration of sustainability. Where appropriate, restoration of damaged caves should be undertaken, rather than opening new caves for tourism

9. Governments should ensure that a representative selection of karst sites is declared as protected areas (especially as category I - IV in Appendix 1) under legislation which provides secure tenure and active management.

10. Priority in protection should be given to areas or sites having high natural, social or cultural value; possessing a wide range of values within the one site; which have suffered minimal environmental degradation; and/or of a type not already represented in the protected areas system of their country.

11. Where possible, a protected area should include the total catchment area of the karst.

12. Where such coverage is not possible, environmental controls or total catchment management agreements under planning, water management or other legislation should be used to safeguard the quantity and quality of water inputs to the karst system.
13. Public authorities should identify karst areas not included within protected areas and give consideration to safeguarding the values of these areas by such means as planning controls, programs of public education, heritage agreements or covenants.
14. Management agencies should seek to develop their expertise and capacity for karst management.
15. Managers of karst areas and specific cave sites should recognise that these landscapes are complex three-dimensional integrated natural systems comprised of rock, water, soil, vegetation and atmosphere elements.
16. Management in karst and caves should aim to maintain natural flows and cycles of air and water through the landscape in balance with prevailing climatic and biotic regimes.
17. Managers should recognise that in karst, surface actions may be sooner or later translated into impacts directly underground or further downstream.
18. Pre-eminent amongst karst processes is the cascade of carbon dioxide from low levels in the external atmosphere through greatly enhanced levels in the soil atmosphere to reduced levels in cave passages. Elevated soil carbon dioxide levels depend on plant root respiration, microbial activity and a healthy soil invertebrate fauna. This cascade must be maintained for the effective operation of karst solution processes.
19. The mechanism by which this is achieved is the interchange of air and water between surface and underground environments. Hence the management of quality and quantity of both air and water is the keystone of effective management at regional, local and site specific scales. Development on the surface must take into account the infiltration pathways of water.
20. Catchment boundaries commonly extend beyond the limits of the rock units in which the karst has formed. The whole karst drainage network should be defined using planned water tracing experiments and cave mapping. It should be recognised that the boundary of these extended catchments can fluctuate dramatically according to weather conditions, and that relict cave passages can be reactivated following heavy rain.
21. More than in any other landscape, a total catchment management regime must be adopted in karst areas. Activities undertaken at specific sites may have wider ramifications in the catchment due to the ease of transfer of materials in karst.

22. Soil management must aim to minimise erosive loss and alteration of soil properties such as aeration, aggregate stability, organic matter content and a healthy soil biota.

23. A stable natural vegetation cover should be maintained as this is pivotal to the prevention of erosion and maintenance of critical soil properties.

24. Establishment and maintenance of karst protected areas can contribute to the protection of both the quality and quantity of groundwater resources for human use. Catchment protection is necessary both on the karst and on contributing non-karst areas. Activities within caves may have detrimental effects on regional groundwater quality.

25. Management should aim to maintain the natural transfer rates and quality of fluids, including gases, through the integrated network of cracks, fissures and caves in the karst. The nature of materials introduced must be carefully considered to avoid adverse impacts on air and water quality.

26. The extraction of rocks, soil, vegetation and water will clearly interrupt the processes that produce and maintain karst, and therefore such uses must be carefully planned and executed to minimise environmental impact. Even the apparently minor activity of removing limestone pavement or other karren for ornamental decoration of gardens or buildings has a drastic impact and should be subject to the same controls as any major extractive industry.

27. Imposed fire regimes on karst should, as far as is practicable, mimic those occurring naturally.

28. While it is desirable that people should be able to visit and appreciate karst features such as caves, the significance and vulnerability of many such features means that great care must be taken to minimise damage, particularly when cumulative over time. Management planning should recognise this fact and management controls should seek to match the visitor population to the nature of the resource.

29. International, regional and national organisations concerned with aspects of karst protection and management should recognise the importance of international co-operation and do what they can to disseminate and share expertise.

30. The documentation of cave and karst protection/management policies should be encouraged, and such policies made widely available to other management authorities.

31. Data bases should be prepared listing cave and karst areas included within protected areas, but also identifying major unprotected areas which deserve recognition. Karst values of existing and potential World Heritage sites should be similarly recorded.

APPENDIX 5

Guidelines (Spanish)

1. La planificación efectiva para regiones cársicas exige una apreciación integral de todos sus valores económicos, científicos y humanos dentro del contexto cultural y político local.

2. La integridad de cualquier sistema cársico depende de una relación interactiva entre la tierra, el aire y el agua. Cualquier interferencia con esta relación probablemente tendrá efectos no deseables y debería estar sujeto a una asesoría ambiental amplia.

3. Los administradores de zonas terrestres deben identificar la cuenca total de cualquier terreno cársico, y estar atentos al impacto potencial de cualquier actividad dentro de la cuenca, aún si dicha actividad no esta localizada dentro del mismo carso.

4. Acciones destructivas en el carso, tales como canteras o la construcción de represas deberían situarse de modo que se minimiza el conflicto con otros recursos o valores intrínsicos.

5. La contaminación de las aguas subterráneas plantea problemas especiales en el carso y siempre debería ser minimizado y sujeto a monitoreo. Este monitoreo debe basarse sobre eventos y no sobre intervalos regulares ya que la mayoría de los contaminantes son transportados a través de sistemas cársicos durante tormentas e inundaciones.

6. Todos los demás usos de áreas cársicas deben planificarse para minimizar los impactos no deseables, y sujetarse a monitoreo para proveer información a la toma de decisiones en el futuro.

7. Además de recononcer la naturaleza no renovabe de muchos fenómenos cársicos, particularmente dentro de las cuevas, la buena administración exige que los fenómenos dañados deben ser restaurados en lo posible.

8. El desarrollo de cuevas con fines turísticos exige planificación cuidadosa que incluye la consideración de la sostenibilidad. Cuando sea apropiado se debería restaurar las cuevas dañadas en vez de abrir nuevas cuevas para el turismo.

9. Los gobiernos deben asegurar que una selección representativa de sitios cársicos sean declarados como áreas protegidas (especialmente como las Categorías I-IV en el Apéndice 1) bajo una legislación que promueve una administración segura y activa.

10. Areas o sitios con un alto valor natural, social o cultural; que posean una amplia gama de valores en un solo sitio; que han sufrido una mínima degradación ambiental; como también de un tipo aún no representado en el sistema de áreas protegidas del país deberían tener la prioridad en la protección.

11. Cuando sea posible, una área protegida debería incluir toda la cuenca del carso.

12. Cuando semejante cobertura no es posible, se debería utilizar otros medios de protección, tales como controles ambientales o reglamentos de administración de la cuenca total, de acuerdo con la legislación vigente sobre planificación, manejo hídrico, o de otro tipo, para salvaguardar la cantidad y calidad de los aportes hídricos al sistema cársico.

13. Las autoridades públicas deben identificar las areas cársicas no incluídas dentro de las zonas protegidas y considerar salvaguardar los valores de estas zonas a través de medios como los controles de planificación, programas de educación al público, o diversos acuerdos como sobre el patrimonio público.

14. Las agencias administrativas deben procurar desarrollar su experiencia y capacidad para el manejo cársico.

15. Los administradores de áreas cársicas y de cuevas aisladas deben reconocer que estos paisajes son complejos sistemas naturales tridimensionales integrados por roca, agua, suelo, vegetación y elementos atmosféricos.

16. La administración de cuevas y carso debe dirigirse al mantenimiento de los flujos y ciclos naturales del aire y agua através del paisaje en equilibrio con los regimenes climáticos y bióticos prevalecientes.

17. Los administradores deben reconocer que en el carso, las acciones sobre la superficie pueden tener un impacto subterráneo directo tarde o temprano.

18. De todos lo procesos cársicos, el flujo del dióxido carbónico, desde concentraciones bajas en la atmósfera externa a través de altos niveles en la atmósfera del suelo hasta los niveles reducidos en las galerías subterráneas, es uno de los mas pre-iminentes. Los niveles elevados de dióxido de carbono en el suelo dependen de la respiracíon radicular vegetal, actividad microbiana y la presencia de una saludable fauna de invertebrados en el suelo. Este flujo debe mantenerse para asegurar una operación efectiva de los procesos disolutivos cársicos.

19. El mecanismo que permite esto es el intercambio del agua y aire entre los ambientes subterráneos y de la superficie. Claramente el manejo, tanto de la cantidad como de la calidad, del aire y del agua sera un fundamento de la administración regional, local y particular. Obras de desarrollo sobre la superficie deben tomar en cuenta las vías de infiltración del agua.

20. Los bordes de la cuencas comunmente se extienden más allá de los límites de las unidades rocosas en las cuales se forma el carso. Toda la red cársica de drenaje debe definirse utilizando ensayos planificados de marcaje de aguas y topografía espeleológica. Se debe reconocer que las fronteras de estas cuencas pueden fluctuar de manera dramática de acuerdo con las condiciones del tiempo y que una galería subterránea muerta puede entrar en actividad después de una fuerte lluvia.

21. En el carso, más que en cualquier otro tipo de paisaje, se debe adoptar un régimen de manejo total de la cuenca. Las actividades que se llevan a cabo en sitios específicos pueden tener mayores ramificaciones en la cuenca debido a la facilidad del transporte de materiales en el carso.

22. El manejo de suelos debe lograr minimizar su pérdida erosiva y la alteración de ciertas propiedades del suelo tales como la aireación, estabilidad de agregados, contenido de materia orgánica y presencia de una biota saludable.

23. Una cobertura vegetal natural y estable debe mantenerse por su papel intrínsico en prevenir la erosión y mantener propiedades críticas del suelo.

24. El establecimiento de áreas protegidas cársicas puede contribuir a la protección tanto de la calidad como de la cantidad de recursos hídricos freáticos para uso humano. La protección de cuencas es necesaria no solamente en las areas sobre el carso sino también sobre las áreas contribuyentes no-cársicas. Las actividades dentro de las cuevas pueden tener efectos detrimentales sobre la calidad de agua a nivel regional.

25. El manejo debe procurar mantener las tasas naturales de transferencia y calidad de los líquidos, incluyendo los gases, a través de la red integral de grietas, fisuras y cuevas en el carso. Se debe cuidadosamente considerar la naturaleza de los materiales que se introducen para evitar impactos adversos sobre la calidad del aire y agua.

26. La extracción de roca, vegetación y agua claramente interrumpirá los procesos que producen y mantienen al carso, y por lo tanto, tales usos deben planificarse cuidadosamente y ejecutarse minimizando el impacto ambiental.

27. Los ciclos de fuego sobre el carso deben seguir los ciclos naturales hasta donde sea posible.

28. Mientras es deseable que la gente pueda visitar y apreciar áreas con caractelísticas cársicas tales como cavernas, la importancia y vulnerabilidad de estos áreas significa que debe ser tomado con mucho cuidado para así minimizar cualquier tipo de daño, particularmente acumulado sobre un largo periodo de tiempo. El plan de manejo debería reconocer este hecho y los controles de manejo deberían tratar de hacer coincidir la cantidad de visitantes con la naturaleza del recurso.

29. Las organizaciones internacionales, regionales y nacionales que se preocupan de la protección y administración del carso deben reconocer la importancia de la cooperación internacional y participar hasta donde sea posible en difundir y compartir conocimientos.

30. La documentación de políticas de protección de cuevas y carso debe alentarse, además de permitir autoridades administrativas ajenas acceso a ellas.

31. Se debe preparar bancos de datos que registren las areas cársicas y las cuevas incluídas dentro de áreas protegidas, además de identificar áreas significativas que merecen protección. Igualmente deben registrarse los valores cársicos de las áreas designadas como 'Herencia Mundial', tanto actuales como en potencia.

APPENDIX 6

Guidelines (French)

RECOMMANDATIONS

1. La gestion efficace des régions karstiques requiert une complète évaluation de toutes leurs valeurs économiques, scientifiques et humaines dans le cadre du contexte culturel et politique local.

2. L'intégrité de tout système karstiue dépend de la relation interactive entre la terre, l'eau et l'air. Toute interférence dans cette relation peut provoquer des effets indésirables et devrait être sujetté à une évolution environnementale complète.

3. Les responsables de l'aménagement du territoire devraient identifier l'intégralite de la zone d'infiltration des eaux de tout terrain karstique et être particulièrement attentifs à l'impact potentiel de toute activité au sein de cette zone d'infiltration, y compris les zones qui ne sont pas directement situées sur le karst.

4. Les activitees destrurtrices du karst telles que l'extraction minière (carrières) ou la construction de barrages, devraient être localisées de manière à permettre de minimiser tout conflit avec d'autres ressources patrimoniales essentielles.

5. La pollution des eaux souterraines pose des problèmes particuliers au karst et devrait toujours être minimisée et contrôlée. Ce contrôle devrait être réellement éfablieté et non simplement promulgée régulièrement et ce tant que les eaux très polluantes créées par orages et inondations seront véhiculées par le système karstique.

6. Toutes les autres utilisations humaines des zones karstiques devraient être planifiées de manière à minimiser les effets indésirables, et être étudiées afin de disposer d' informations pour les décisions futures.

7. Tout en reconnaissant le caractère "non_renouvelable" de nombreuses caractéristiques du karst, particulièrement en ce qui concerne les grottes, une bonne gestion implique que les dégâts soient restaurés dans la mesure du possible.

8. L'expansion des grottes à fins touristiques demande des programmes bien pensés, ainsi qu'un important soutien. Où serait nécessaire, la restoration de grottes endommagées devrait être prise en charge plutôt que d'offrir aux touristes l'accès à de nouveaux sites.

9. Les gouvernements devraient s'assurer d'une sélection représentative des sites karstiques déclarés zones protégées (spécialement pour catégories I - IV appendice 1) dans le cadre des législations qui stipulent des activités sûres et une réelle direction.

10. Une priorité de protection devrait être attribuéeu aix zones ou sites présentant une grande valeur naturelle, sociale ou culturelle; possédant un large éventail de valeurs différentes au sein d'un même site; n'ayant souffert que d'une dégradation environnementale minimum; et/ou d'un type encore non représenté dans les zones protégées du pays.

11. Dans la mesure du possible, la totalité de la zone dínfiltration des eaux devrait être incluse dans la zone protégée.

12. Lá oú une telle protection n'est pas possible, un contrôle environnemental, un contrat de gestion de la zone d'infiltration devrait être envisagés dans le cadre de lois sur l'aménagement du territoire ou sur la gestion des eaux afin de préserver la quantité et la qualité de l'alimentation en eau du système karstique.

13. Les autorités publiques devraient identifier les zones karstiques qui ne sont pas incluses dans les zones protégées et prendre des mesures pour la sauvegarde des caractéritiques patrimoniales de ces zones par des moyens tels que contrôles de gestion, campagnes de sensibilisation du public, accords patrimoniaux ou conventions.

14. Les différents organismes responsables de la gestion du territoire devraient développer leur connaissance du milieu karstique.

15. Les autorités responsables des zones karstiques et des sites souterrains et individuels devraient reconnaître que les terrains représentent un système intégré tridimensionnel complexe constitué de roche, d'eau, de terre, de végétation et d'éléments atmosphériques.

16. La gestion du karst et des grottes devrait avoir pour objectif de maintenir l'écoulement et le cycle de l'air et de l'eau à travers le massif de manière équilibrée par rapport aux régimes climatiques et biotiques prédominants.

17. Les gestionnaires devraient reconnaître que, dans le karst, toute action en surface peut rapidement se traduire par un impact sous terre ou enavaldu flux.

18. Le passage du taux de gaz carbonique d'un faible niveau dans l'atmosphère de surface a un niveau trés augmenté dans l'atmosphère du sol puis à un niveau réduit dans les cavités souterraines représente un phénomène essentiel dans le processus karstique. Le niveau élevé en gaz carbonique de sol dépend de la respication des cacines des plantes, de l'activité microbienne et de la bonne santé de la faune invertébrée du sol. Ce phénomène doit être maintenu pour conserver un processus de karstification efficace.

19. Le mécanisme permettant ce phénomène est réalisé par l'échange d'air et d'eau entre la surface et l'environnement souterrain. Ceci implique que la gestion de la qualité et de la quantité aussi bien de l'air que de l'eau est la clé d'une gestion efficace tant au niveau régional que local ou d'un site individuel. Tout développement en surface doit prendre en compte les chemins d'infiltration des eaux.

20. La zone d' infiltrations des eaux s'étend généralement au-delà des limites de la zone karstique. L' ensemble du système d'infiltration des eaux devrait être défini par des expériences de colorations planifiées et de la topographie des grottes. I devrait être pris en compte que les limites de cette zone peuvent varier très sérieusement selon les conditions météorologiques incluisant une réactivitée de certaines cavités après de lourdes pluies.

21. Plus que pour tout autre terrain, une politique de gestion globale du système d'infiltration des eaux doit être adoptée dans les zones karstiques. Toute activité entreprise sur un site spécifique peut avoir des implications sur le système d'infiltration étant donné la facilité de transfert des substances à travers le karst.

22. La gestion du territoire doit avoir pour objectif de minimiser les pertes et altérations de propriétés du sol, telles qu' aération, agglomération stable, contenu organique et santé du biotope, dues á l'érosion.

23. Une couche végétale stable, naturelle devrait être essentielle dans la prévention de l'érosion et dans la conservation des propriétés indispensables du sol.

24. L'établissement et la conservation de zones karstiques protégées peut contribuer à la protection de la qualité et de la quantité des ressources en eau potable souterraine pour l'utilisation humaine. La protection des zones d'infiltration est nécessaire aussi bien sur les zones karstiques qui contribuent à celte infiltration. Les activités dans les grottes peuvent avoir un impact au détriment de la qualité de l'eau potable souterraine dans la région.

25. Les gestionnaires devraient avoir pour obectif de maintenir le taux de transfert des fluides,y compris de gaz, à travers le réseau intégré de failles, fissures et grottes dans le karst. La nature des substances introduites doit être soigneusement considérée afin d'évitrer tout impact négatif sur la qualité de l'air et de l'eau.

26. L'extraction de roche, de sol, de végétation et d'eau va clairement interrompre le processus qui crée et conserve le karst, il faut cependant que de telles exploitations soient soigneusement planifiées, et exécutées de manière á minimiser l'impact environnemental. L'apparente extraction mineure de plaques de chaux et autres matériaux karstiques usités pour l'aggrément des jardins ou en tant que matériaux de construction affecte réellement le karst. C'est pourquoi elle devrait être soumise à des contrôles aux même titres que toute autre extraction miniere.

27. La fréquence des incendies volontaires sur les zones karstiques devrait, dans la mesure du possible, correspondre a celle qui surviendrait naturellement.

28. Bien qu'il soit souhaitable que le public ait la possibilité de visiter et d'apprécier les phénomènes karstiques tels que les grottes, l'impotance et la vulnérabilité d'un grand nombre de ces phénomènes implique que la plus grande prudence doit être prise afin de minimiser les déteriorations, tout particulièrement lorsque celles-ci se répètent dans le temps. Les autorités devraient reconnaître ce fait et prendre des mesures de contrôle afin d'adapter la fréquentation à la nature du site.

29. Les organisations internationales, régionales et nationales concernées par les différents aspects de la protection du karst devraient reconnaître l'importance de la coopération internationale et faire des efforts pour distribuer et partager leurs expériences.

30. Le collecte d'informations sur la réglementation pour la protection et la gestion des grottes et du karst devrait être encouragée, et ces informations devraient être accessibles à toutes les autorités responsables.

31. Une banque de données devrait être établie afin de répertorier les grottes et les zones karstiques déjà inclues dans le cadre de zones protégées mais, également, identifiant les principales zones "non-protégées"qui mériteraient de bénéficier d'une telle protection. Les sites karstiques inscrits à la liste du Patrimoine Mondial, ou méritant de l'être, devraient également être répertoriés.